ALL ABOUT INSECTS

ALL ABOUT COCKROACHES

by Golriz Golkar

pogo

Ideas for Parents and Teachers

Pogo Books let children practice reading informational text while introducing them to nonfiction features such as headings, labels, sidebars, maps, and diagrams, as well as a table of contents, glossary, and index.

Carefully leveled text with a strong photo match offers early fluent readers the support they need to succeed.

Before Reading

- "Walk" through the book and point out the various nonfiction features. Ask the student what purpose each feature serves.
- Look at the glossary together. Read and discuss the words.

Read the Book

- Have the child read the book independently.
- Invite him or her to list questions that arise from reading.

After Reading

- Discuss the child's questions. Talk about how he or she might find answers to those questions.
- Prompt the child to think more. Ask: Have you ever seen a cockroach? Where was it?

Pogo Books are published by Jump!
5357 Penn Avenue South
Minneapolis, MN 55419
www.jumplibrary.com

Library of Congress Cataloging-in-Publication Data

Names: Golkar, Golriz, author.
Title: All about cockroaches / by Golriz Golkar.
Description: Minneapolis, MN: Jump!, Inc., [2025]
Series: All about insects | Includes index.
Audience: Ages 7-10
Identifiers: LCCN 2023050493 (print)
LCCN 2023050494 (ebook)
ISBN 9798889969815 (hardcover)
ISBN 9798889969822 (paperback)
ISBN 9798889969839 (ebook)
Subjects: LCSH: Cockroaches–Juvenile literature.
Cockroaches–Life cycles–Juvenile literature.
Classification: LCC QL505.5 .G655 2025 (print)
LCC QL505.5 (ebook)
DDC 595.7/28–dc23/eng/20231204
LC record available at https://lccn.loc.gov/2023050493
LC ebook record available at https://lccn.loc.gov/2023050494

Editor: Katie Chanez
Designer: Emma Almgren-Bersie

Photo Credits: Dejawu/Shutterstock, cover; 7th Son Studio/Shutterstock, 1; Nynke van Holten/Shutterstock, 3; ErikKarits/iStock, 4; pedphoto36pm/iStock, 5; blickwinkel/Alamy, 6-7; UlrikaArt/Shutterstock, 8; acarapi/Shutterstock, 9; Protasov AN/Shutterstock, 9 (inset); D. Kucharski K. Kucharska/Shutterstock, 10-11; gan chaonan/Shutterstock, 12-13 (foreground), 18-19; Svetlana Makarova/iStock, 12-13 (background); RealityImages/Shutterstock, 14-15tl; smuay/iStock, 14-15tr; Zanthra/iStock, 14-15bl; RHJ/iStock, 14-15br, 20-21; Portographer/Shutterstock, 16; Hafiez Razali/Shutterstock, 17; rdegrie/iStock, 23.

Printed in the United States of America at Corporate Graphics in North Mankato, Minnesota.

TABLE OF CONTENTS

CHAPTER 1

CRAWLING COCKROACH

An **insect** crawls with six thin legs. It is shaped like an oval. Two **antennas** feel and smell. What is it? It is a cockroach!

There are more than 4,500 cockroach **species**. They like warm, wet, and dark places. They are **pests**. Why? They sneak into homes. They eat any food they find. They are hard to get rid of.

Males usually have two pairs of wings. Females often have none. All cockroaches have two cerci. They are on the back of the body. They look like short antennas. These help cockroaches sense their surroundings.

TAKE A LOOK!

What are the parts of a cockroach? Take a look!

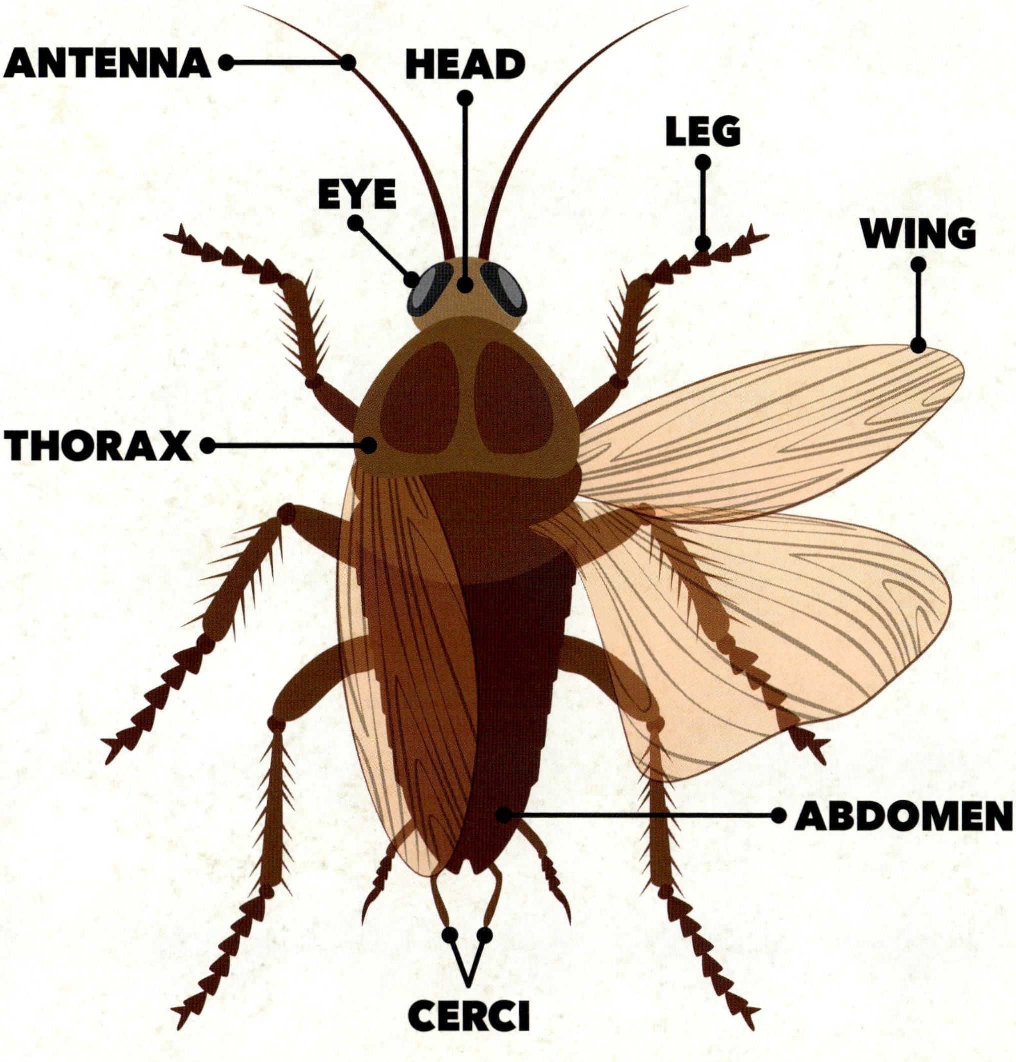

CHAPTER 2

LIFE CYCLE

Adult cockroaches **mate**. A female makes an egg case. It is called an **ootheca**. It looks like a bean!

Each one holds between 10 and 50 eggs. Some females carry the egg cases. Others hide them in safe places.

After one to three months, **nymphs** hatch. They **molt** many times. They grow each time. Nymphs are white when they molt. Then they turn brown or gray.

TAKE A LOOK!

Cockroaches grow in four stages. Take a look!

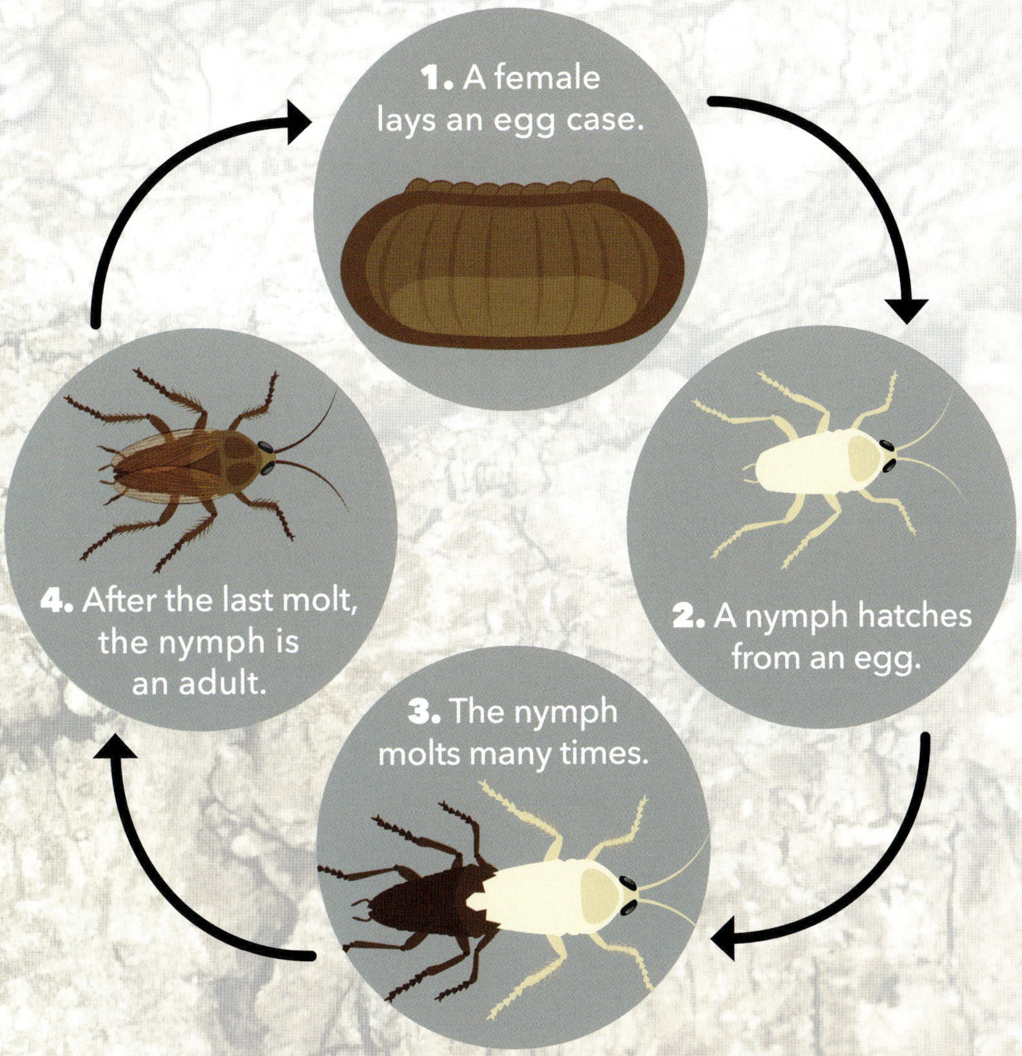

After 40 to 160 days, they molt one last time. They become adults. They are their final size and color. Some have wings. But they are not very good fliers.

DID YOU KNOW?

Cockroaches are one of Earth's oldest insects. They have been around for more than 100 million years. They were around when dinosaurs lived!

brown-banded cockroach

German cockroach

oriental cockroach

American cockroach

Adults live up to one year. They spend their time eating. Different cockroaches like different foods. Brown-banded cockroaches like glue and other sticky materials. German cockroaches like sweet and floury foods. Oriental cockroaches like plants and garbage. American cockroaches will eat almost anything!

DID YOU KNOW?

Cockroaches can live about one month without food. They can even live up to one week without a head!

CHAPTER 3

CREEPY CRAWLIES

Cockroaches are **prey** for some animals. Mice, frogs, spiders, lizards, and beetles eat them.

Cockroaches hide during the day. They sleep in dark places. They come out at night. They look for food.

Cockroaches **shed** skin as they move. They spread waste. They spread **bacteria**, too. This can make people sick. Yuck!

Cockroaches can live in almost any **environment**. Ones found outside can be left alone. Ones found inside should be removed. Have you ever seen a cockroach?

DID YOU KNOW?

When a cockroach's cerci feel movement nearby, they signal the legs to move. The cockroach quickly crawls away. This is why they are hard to catch!

ACTIVITIES & TOOLS

TRY THIS!

CUTOUT COCKROACH

Make a cockroach in this fun activity!

What You Need:

- 2 sheets of black construction paper
- pencil
- scissors
- 4 black pipe cleaners
- clear tape
- glue
- 2 large googly eyes

1. **Draw a large oval on one sheet of construction paper. Cut it out. This is the cockroach's body. Draw a line near its neck. Above the line is the cockroach's head.**
2. **Cut two pipe cleaners into six pieces. Tape three pieces to each side of the body. Bend the pipe cleaners. These are the legs.**
3. **Draw two ovals on the other sheet of paper. Make them smaller than the body. Cut them out. These are the wings.**
4. **Make a V with the wings. Glue them together. Then glue the tip of the V to the top of the body.**
5. **Cut one pipe cleaner in half. Tape each half to the head. These are the antennas.**
6. **Cut two small pieces off the last pipe cleaner. Glue them to the bottom of the body. These are the cerci.**
7. **Glue two googly eyes to the head. Now you have a cockroach!**

GLOSSARY

antennas: Feelers on the head of an insect.

bacteria: Tiny living things found everywhere.

environment: The natural surroundings of living things, such as the air, land, or sea.

insect: A small animal with three pairs of legs, one or two pairs of wings, and three main body parts.

mate: To come together to produce babies.

molt: To shed an old, outer skin so that a new one can grow.

nymphs: Young cockroaches in the larvae stage.

ootheca: A tough egg case laid by a female cockroach.

pests: Insects or animals that interfere with human activity.

prey: Animals that are hunted by other animals for food.

shed: To lose, get rid of, or let something fall.

species: One of the groups into which similar animals and plants are divided.

INDEX

TO LEARN MORE

Finding more information is as easy as 1, 2, 3.

1. Go to www.factsurfer.com
2. Enter "cockroaches" into the search box.
3. Choose your book to see a list of websites.

FACT SURFER